Bicycles

For Ben and John

First published in North America in 2006 by Two-Can Publishing
11571 K-Tel Drive, Minnetonka, MN 55343
www.two-canpublishing.com

A portion of the proceeds from this book will benefit Oxfam GB.

Oxfam would like to acknowledge, with thanks, the following photographers:
Annie Bungeroth (pages 5 and 10–11), Howard Davies (pages 24–25 and cover), Julio Etchart (pages 12–13),
Jim Holmes (pages 6–7, 14–15 and 20–21), Ley Honor Roberts (pages 8–9), Crispin Hughes (pages 16–17),
Rhodri Jones (pages 22–23 and back cover), Sean Sprague (pages 26–27) and Penny Tweedie (pages 18–19).

The book begins on page 6.

First published in Great Britain in 2006 by Frances Lincoln Children's Books
4 Torriano Mews, Torriano Avenue, London NW5 2RZ
www.franceslincoln.com

Library of Congress Cataloging-in-Publication Data on file

ISBN 1-58728-529-0 (HC)
ISBN 1-58728-530-4 (PB)

Printed in China

1 2 3 4 5 10 09 08 07 06

Bicycles

Kate Petty

in association with

Linh can ride his mother's bike, but it is much too big for him. She won't let him ride on the busy road that runs through his village in Vietnam.

I have to stand up to reach the pedals!

When Lucy's family goes for a bike ride, she rides in a trailer. Their favorite bike path in the United Kingdom used to have train tracks on it.

I can't wait to ride a bike by myself!

Grandma Rose from Malawi uses a bike in her work. She is riding to the market to sell a big can of milk.

It's easier to carry heavy things with a bike.

Cidinha has plenty of room to play. She lives next door to a soccer field in her village in Brazil. She is using a bicycle wheel as a toy.

It's hard to keep the wheel rolling!

Mumi and her friend live on the island of Java. They are fixing her bicycle chain. It came off on the bumpy road.

I'll have to oil the chain when I get home.

These three boys are coming home from school in Kenya. A bike taxi will take them across the river to their neighborhood.

This is the quickest way to get home!

Alexis lives in Alice Springs, in the Australian desert. She has a big family, so it's nice to get away on her bike sometimes.

It's fun to take my mountain bike off-road!

Kamalotas likes to ride her bike with her dad on the weekend. It's a good way to explore her hometown in Thailand.

This street is nice and shady.

Dramane can't wait to get his bicycle fixed. He lives in Mali, where there is lots of space to ride around.

This bike was a present from my dad.

Lots of children ride their bikes to this school in Cambodia. They come early so they can eat breakfast before class begins.

We will race each other home after school!

Tomasa has a good use for a bicycle! She uses parts of it to spin thread for weaving. She belongs to a group of weavers in Guatemala.

The money I earn will buy a new dress.

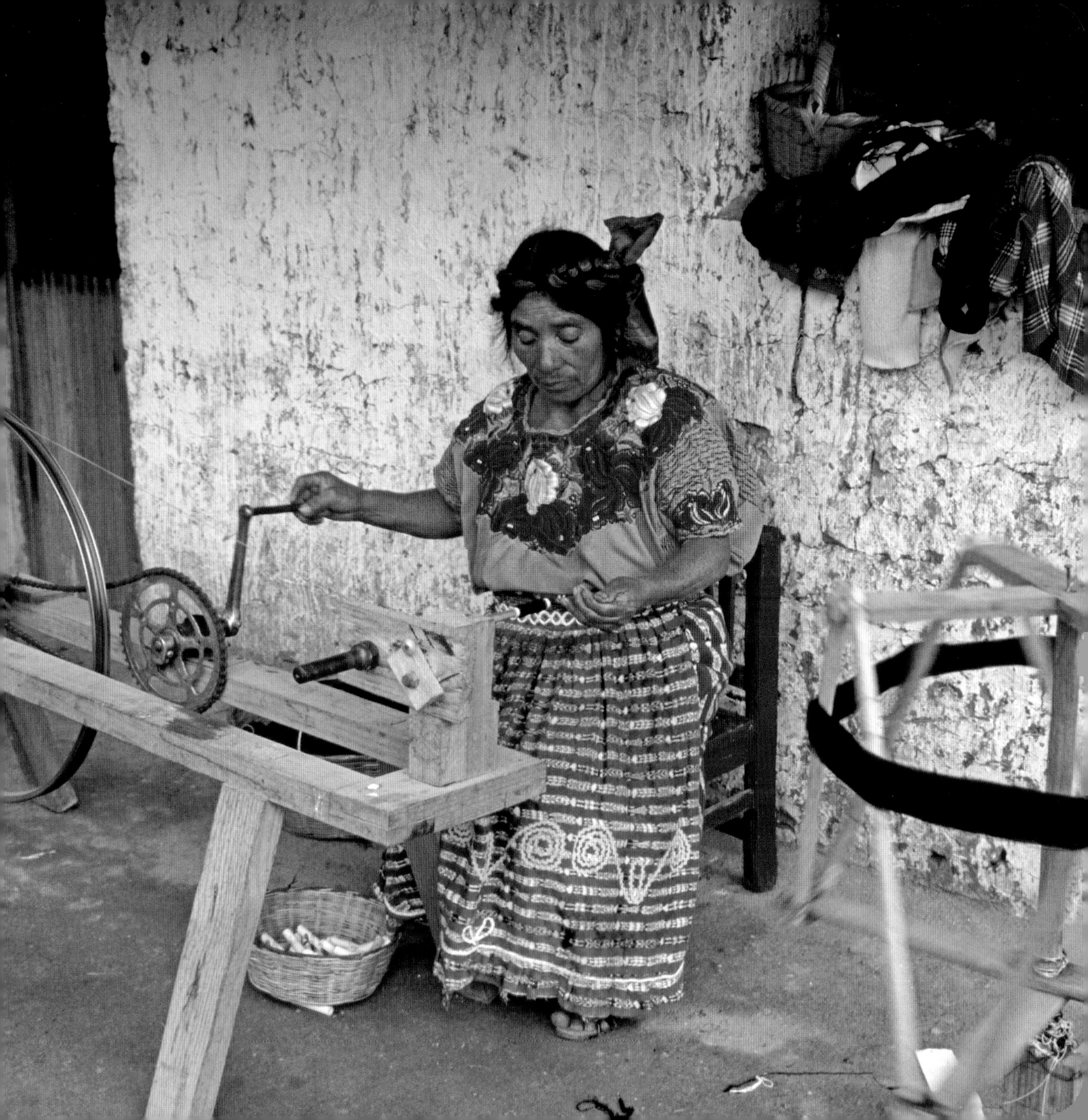

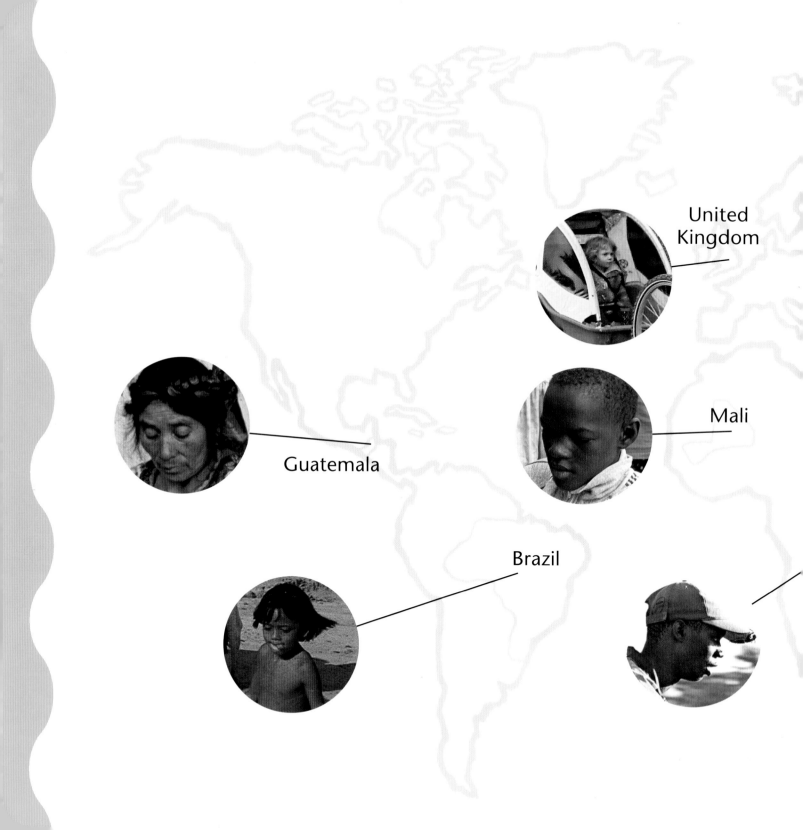

United
Kingdom

Guatemala

Mali

Brazil

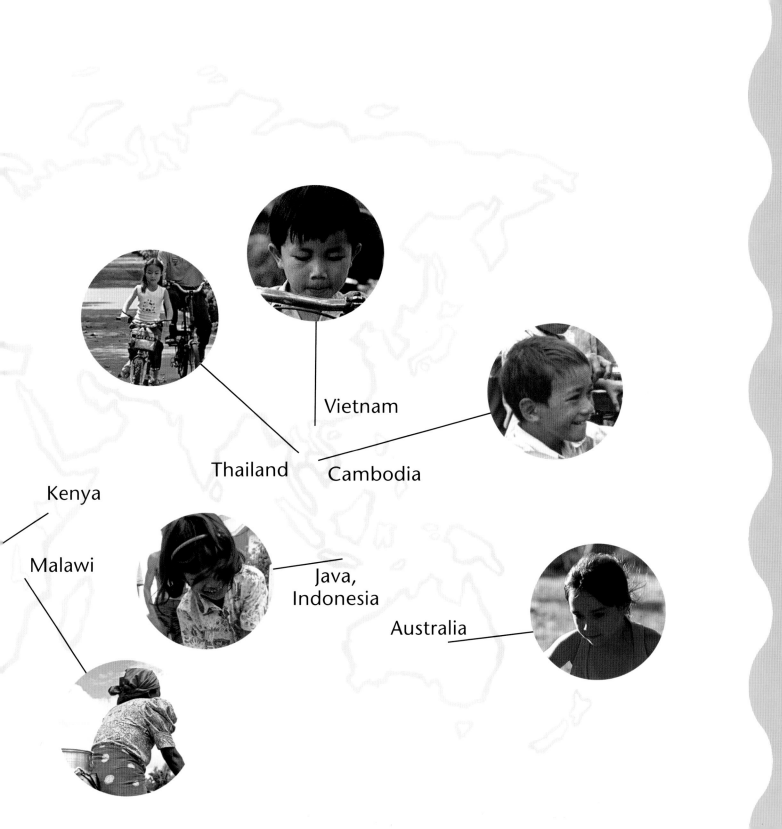

Vietnam

Thailand

Cambodia

Kenya

Malawi

Java,
Indonesia

Australia